ANTHOLOGY OF POEMS

Mutiat T. Adebowale

authorHOUSE®

AuthorHouse™ UK Ltd.
500 Avebury Boulevard
Central Milton Keynes, MK9 2BE
www.authorhouse.co.uk
Phone: 08001974150

First published by AuthorHouse 3/29/2010

ISBN: 978-1-4520-0400-6 (sc)

This book is printed on acid-free paper.

DEDICATION

This book is dedicated to
the glory of Almighty God.

INTRODUCTION

This anthology of poems consists of various types and forms of poems.

They are general poems, in English language with no specification to particular gender, race, or religion. They are poems for all people who love simple poetic thoughts.

They are the original poetic rendition of an individual, based on experiences, thoughts and inspirations.

CONTENTS

TROUBLES IN LOVE

Loving, though wonderful,

Difficult to know who to love

Shattered dreams may be

Love shall crawl through

Infatuations! Deceits!

Arise for true love is gone

Cupboard love in town, with policy

Ride on the coat-tails

Lovers made down

For their loved ones are gone

Carried away,

Oh! So far away

Carried away by booted sophistication

But alas! True love shall find its place

And know it,

That lucky, I call it, the soul that is loved

With honesty, care and patience

For it is rear around.

ODE TO BUNMI OYELEKE AKANNI (BOA)

Beyond you have gone

To rest and not to mourn

To be free from palsy hands shaking each other

You have left this world, where fret and fever give order

In the bosom of our lord you shall lie forever

Though pains were yours but never

Sleep well love,

In the hands of our lord above

You have left us and gone

In this world to suffer for long

We looked up to you for our success

But you've left us to nonsense

You that never allowed us to suffer,

You are gone and we are scattered like orphans

We shed bitter tears

For it is hard to bear

Our dreams are shattered

And our days, scattered

If only you could come back to life,

That you live, some will friend the knife

How we wish you see us

To record for us our loss

Rest in the bosom of our lord our love,

In the deem sky above

You have left us your good deeds

Forever to satisfy our needs

For your spirit shall see us through our
undertakings

And crown success our makings

We would strive, seek, find and not to yield

To make your name fall, sink die not, but always to
lead

Rest in perfect peace, my dear

For you'll always be there.

DARK DAY

My heart aches and bleeds so hard

For sourness has overwhelmed a day in my life

Dutifully I acted

Only for my labour to be in vain

Woefully, I shed bitter tears

I am shattered

A finger into the mouth,

Onto the floor, it was bitten

I am sad and bad

Those I loved and respected

Make mockery of my whole

My heart is cracked, as the shells of an egg

Crushed in the hands of giants

Deep in me, I know sorrow

Mute and muffled a maid

Where to turn, I find not

But for a day,

Truth wilt out

And joyful shall thou soul again.

DON'T SAY WE ARE POOR

When living comes with pain

Pain of uneasiness

Pain of uncertainties

Don't say we are poor

Spartan, never rosy

Don't say we are poor

Poverty so many colours

Not the first house on the lane lays all beauty

Nay, the most beautiful house filled with true beauties

Don't say we are poor

Though wealthily healthy

Never healthy in health

Don't say we are poor

All riches may scram to nought

Worthless befalling

Futile its existence

(continues)

When no peace of mind prevails

How shall I spend my money?

Is it riches without honour?

Moral virtue comes none

Godliness and goodness follows

What fate lays our both?

When a clicking pauper

Takes my dues

Don't say you are poor

Poverty oh! So many colours.

THE LEADING LIGHT

The years roll on

The days pass by

Then the clock struck!

I never knew I will see the light

It little wonders me

If I will crawl through my darkness

But alas! My heart rejoices

The water flows onto my veins

And runs my flowing blood blue

And my hot feet cool

I hooked a right one

In hands to a place I admire

A bite of everlasting joy I tasted

Oh! Sweet day.

GREYING DAYS

My heart aches and bleeds

Though as if my sun shall rise not,

In the east but west

I look up to my grey hair

And lo! Displease I call it

The storm blows relentlessly

And afar it blew my days

A clock or two will wait not

For me,

To pack my luggage

And set out for my long, long journey.

On land or ashore

I pray I smile and laugh at last

But done not by mouth

With prayers, power and pity

To make my hays when bright sun shines,

And let my star be in ascendant

Sometime to come.

MY WORDS

In my words I lay my rest

In my words I shed my tears

My words you alone, is my grip

My words in you my joy is filled

My words, on you, my sorrow is deep

My words, I open to laugh

My words, with you not, I want to part.

My words I yell today

For with creeds, our souls, they want us torn

My words wake up to save

My words reach out to them

My words knock them terror

My words make me show

My words, great me in thy face

My words, today by your brightness

Let us see light

And cramp in the darkness of their nights

In my words I pray I merry.

OH! HOW I LOVE YOU

My heart sings of joy and happiness

When I know I have you

My soul rejoices, for you are mine

I love you with all my heart, my might and my life

My love for you cannot be described

Not for all that loves

Oh! Fervid, that, I call my love for you

It's like honey in sour milk

As hard as a rock,

That has been on crust for ages

I can't afford to lose you

Not for a blink

Just like the queen moon

Among a galaxy of stars, my love for you

What an ardent love, with a difference

Wherever I tread your thoughts always with me

For now, and in the world beyond, I will forever love you

All I do, I cherish your kind.

SONGS OF LAMENTATION

It covers me top all

My head spins round and round

The city a hell on heart

So narrow for us to tread the path

The leaders besiege the space

Our minds may never know care

When our tummies rumble

And our tongues cry for weeds

They shout us down

Our pockets run out of use

And our hatchets lay on strike

They snub and scorn us

We toil hard

Times turn stiff

In the hierarchy, we wave the top

What a nagging ache in my house hold

For all I get is loathe for love

Desires that the ink will run dry

Sickness be whelm my brains

And my temperature escapes

My future is bleak, all is blighted

Indecisive I turn

Worthless my existence

The thought to part my works

Heavens I cry deep unto you

I shout loud to your ears

Hear me if you hear

Save my fate and pave my face

From their fires they ruin

The winds of time and change

Let it blow not my destiny

Make the tide go not with my fortunes

And hold me that I may not descend with my
desires

The work of my strength

The strength of my energy,

The gift I love.

Cease my drums stopping mid-way

I should lead it highest ever

And they should say

Laudable the one you call

For He has led you right

MY LITTLE BIRD THING

As I was going to the stairs

My steps were steep

Slow and still

I saw a little bird thing sly

It perched at my door space

A little boy asked, as in wonder I stare

Do you want it stay?

It's beautiful, it's charming and sweet

It glitters in my eyes so

Its colours a thing of joy to say

How stiff it is, my heart sings

To have it stay and go no long speed

One step, two steps, and away it flew by the third step

See it fly, whispered something

 In the empty space above it swims

Where you can never see

Will I ever catch it smile?

I ponder and I sob

For the colours in my eyes will not seize

The purple it sparkles

I will never forget the silver

In black and white the body is stripped

The tail fan out with grey so sleek,

White, black and silver shining.

Will it go forever and I am sombre?

YET AGAIN

Time has failed, yet it moves

Life is here, still we expect

Years have rolled, the waters of sobs

Won't stop the gush

Life is unkind

From the blood of the womb

The spree is agony

Whence life born,

Bitter the taste as we hope

An empty hope we kept living on

Long gone, today may be well,

Though land unknown.

The first ages, was pain

Pain yet, know no bounds

For sorrow whose tears would come in shapes

If in death, time ago, all pains flown

In here, still melancholy

It is ill fate

The bad luck pierces my heart

Time and again, not any better.

TIDE SO SOON

The ache in my head is fierce
 The tears in my eyes roll fears
The strain of my muscles pulls me hard
The strength of my soul sways like a card
The delusion I know, is not of aggression
Neither for revenge of frustration
The fury of my silence is my regret
My tears of solitude is the object
That I can find no way
 And in limbo I lay
My failing identity leaves me poorly
The absence of true life is sickly
Whether here or there I know not
Here is no longer where it ought
So hot hardly can bear
And no air, can I hear
In my silence I know solitude
For a dashed hope I take refuge
Such that my soul deserves not
But its resistance I can't slot
In my silence there is pain
On me, the tide has made its gain.

MY INSPIRATION

My inspiration lies within

Bears in you quite hidden

For you do not know

I see, and in it I glow

Pervades the insinuations

Which I carry its limitations

Thoughts of our deeds

Will ever remain as leads

You give the energy to stand

With though a thin breath on my hand

Your deep strength of power

And a touch so strong it showers

Such so hard to resist

In your valour you insist

And in that the trust resides

For on it alone, the hope to strive abides

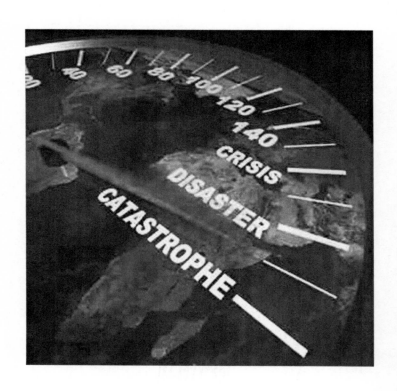

A POEM FOR PEACE

When the walls come cracking

And the children wailing

All girls and boys shouting

The women are fainting

The blast is sounding

And the chaos looming

In the centre of a war pending

The smiles of humanity ending

Some men are hiding

Thoughts of their children dying

Other men do the blasting

With heavy arms destroying

The milk in the heart is drying

The veins of comrades are shedding

Waters of destruction unrelenting

Love, mercy and pity fast vanishing

The crowd is dispersing

(continues)

And the centre not holding

The devil is within and laughing

Ideals of brotherhood is perishing

Will it continue forever unending?

For today's doings

Tomorrow's misdeeds, surely appalling

Innocent children are suffering

The blood spill truly unforgiving

The earth is soiled and decaying

With human blood sorrowing

Let some true joy come rising

And hands be holding

For unity to start living

On the land of the beings.

FROM THIS HOUSE TOP

From this house top I see girls

I see men and women

From this house top I see mockery

Empty mockery I hope

From this house top I see temptation

I see failures and trials

From this house top

I know it   being arduous

I hope success lays it rest

From this house top tolerance is key

I see too, patience to be put

From this house top I see pride

I hope peace returns to the soul

From this house top I see dejection

I see jealousy and envy

From this house top I see rejection

Perhaps it may bring accord

From this house top I see strength

I see faithfulness and dedication

I see a whole new world of change

If only I search the bond and be a sage.

WAKE UP

That is the barn that I peeped through

Look at the sky so blue

The ground I swept yet dirty

Wasted energy feels so   guilty

Recounting my toil

I see the bareness in the soil

I thought I had thrived

But my labour deprived

The lands of my ancestors

My dreams, I hope it restores

All day I work to reap something

Yet I have achieved nothing

The continent of my forefathers

Wake up from your slumber

If we die in chains

You will weigh the gains

For greed in the lane

Our advancement its bane

Let not delusion sink our nation

In this you have carved a foundation

Tongues are wagging

Blood is dripping

Your people are crying

The torture is penetrating

Give us life, to rise and reach

A world of timeless breed

Time has gone past

Let's shed the days of doom cast

To live a world of glory and honour

Which you alone can such   harbour

THE NIGHT

The night, still, quite and empty

You are a darkness I cannot hold

You are dark, oh so black

Traces of white, smoky stuff

Cease in my eyes, each minute I peer

Your darkness I admire

The beauty in your silence

I can't but gasp

A dark black beauty you are

Rolls thought in me

Create shades in my sense

Of fear, despair and cowardice

But the calm in your endurance

Of tomorrow coming

Yet so long it may take

Some stars to pull near

And the sun of the day that will break

Can only give but hope

It's you, it's the night, it's you I dread.

WHAT CAN YOU DO?

What can you do?

Make your fingers grow even?

Mould your head most lovely?

Let your words visible?

Or your fate much florid!

Maybe you think you're wild, weird or wide

Take my life and make it

Build my liver blood stained

let my heart shiver, then I quiver

filter the seas and make salt-free

why don't you quieten sea tide, and

make stagnant waters flow over bank

The mountains let them skip

The rainfall sing, sunshine shed tears

Why not paint me with the moon,

And tie me round with the wind?

The blue sky, the day, and the night?

Think 'bout all these

You know WHAT?

JUST SAY, THANK YOU!

LOST TIE

Thoughts of the wind blow

Gush and rush it went

Never expected neither envisaged

Two playing birds

Now no more

An incursion came

Abruptly it did too

Either bird never sensed

And when it did they called no wrought

With steps so fast, no noise it appeared

Like the waves it moved

Snatched away a bird and snapped

Other frowned but weak

Swears and curses it rained

No ant did this move

Till this date, the gap is lost

And the tie has rotted

A LETTER TO THE BRETHREN

The cry of horror that struck

I looked at the screen

It was a struggle for safety

The lady yelled to save a brother

And I rebuked it

For I want no horror befall my brothers

But aside that

I felt the pinch

The punch that I have missed my brothers

For so, so long

The pain that I not know

When I will see my brothers

The intense love I knew

The tie that marriage has broken

I wept for I love my brothers

But I have not kept my promises

Promises that now surpass me

(continues)

Promises I can only hope fulfil

If life and time permits me

Promises I hold so close to my heart

Promises that breaks me to tears

So much, each time it flickers

I will strive to keep my promise

Of a one true loving sister

Life has failed me to keep

I swear I love my brothers

Just as I did before now

The brothers I knew when I was a girl

With experiences no circumstances can take away

My brothers in the days of rage and fury

All to be back and lie sombre

My brothers of blood and flesh

With no limit to the happiness we shared

Oh! brethren

How life turns only can I care

Poking me is the guilt my heart bears.

IF WISHES WERE MORE

If wishes were more

Oh! Dear, wished your pains snore

And in its sleeping pore

Cease forever its very sore

The agony of old age

Lies on your frailly image

I see you once like me

Forceful and brave

You once had courage your slave

How fair, life can be?

So old with less hope

Helplessness grows along the slope

Wished I could do more

Think of you young, pretty without a bore

I look of you agile and able

Time has failed you now, oh! Feeble

Failed you of those bones and muscles

That once pivoted your never relenting vessel

I can only wish you get some strength

Maybe one to keep your breath

Just till you reckon with death

Only if wishes were more!

THE LAST BREATH

When my steps get weak

And my sight turns bleak

My gaze runs deem

Leaving me a blur dream

I know no more the need

The rest is of the sprout of a seed

Taking solace in the peace

Once torn my heart in piece

The toil of my palm

Now the deeds of a soothing balm

I lay on it my earth

On which I remember the birth

Now leading back the last breath

Through a journey called death.

TOLL OF TIME

There I laid, helplessly astounded

Felt it was someone else

Could it be me? I whispered

Through the window

Peered a neighbour

At the sound of the gun for which I fell

A lad his down, he shouted

Two more to go they proclaimed

Off they ran past the patio

And over the fence they flew

The son of a mother is dying

He is Jane's brother

And daddy wept profusely

What have we done to deserve this?

Just as my blood gush unreservedly

Forming streams of unending sorrow

We watch our community break to its ruins

The neighbour moaned

The destiny and the future of an entity

Washes away before its very presence

The binding love jolts

All on a rivalry, only for blood spilling

I hear the whisper of a voice

Saying

The aggression you feel

Will never melt away

Until a time

When you choose to live above it

And rise beyond the subdues

Of your feelings imbued

Saturated your chaste mind

Only for an unconfined displacements.

Now the mark of a destruction unending

Results to a vengeance propelling"

Could I have taken charge?

If ever comes a second chance.

Lightning Source UK Ltd.
Milton Keynes UK
26 September 2010

160393UK00001B/6/P